WEATHER
—AND—
CLIMATE

VOLUME 10

John Bassett

GROLIER
EDUCATIONAL

Published 2002 by Grolier Educational
Sherman Turnpike,
Danbury, Connecticut 06816

For information address the publisher:
Grolier Educational, Sherman Turnpike,
Danbury, Connecticut 06816

FOR BROWN PARTWORKS

Project editor:	Lisa Magloff
Deputy editor:	Jane Scarsbrook
Text editors:	Caroline Beattie, Lesley Campbell-Wright
Designer:	Joan Curtis
Picture researcher:	Liz Clachan
Illustrations:	Darren Awuah, Mark Walker
Index:	Kay Ollerenshaw
Design manager:	Lynne Ross
Production manager:	Matt Weyland
Managing editor:	Bridget Giles
Editorial director:	Anne O'Daly
Consultant:	Donald R. Franceschetti, PhD University of Memphis

Printed and bound in Hong Kong

Set ISBN 0-7172-5608-1
Volume ISBN 0-7172-5618-9

Library of Congress Cataloging-in-Publication Data
Science Activities / Grolier Educational
        p. cm.
    Includes index.
    Contents: v.1. Electricity and magnetism—v.2. Everyday Chemistry—v.3. Force and motion—v.4. Heat and energy—v.5. Inside matter—v.6. Light and color—v.7. Our Environment—v.8. Sound and hearing—v.9. Using materials—v.10. Weather and climate.
    ISBN 0-7172-5608-1 (set : alk.paper)—ISBN 0-7172-5609-X (v.1 : alk. paper)—ISBN 0-7172-5610-3 (v.2 : alk. paper)—ISBN 0-7172-5611-1 (v.3 : alk. paper)—ISBN 0-7172-5612-X (v.4 : alk. paper)—ISBN 0-7172-5613-8 (v.5 : alk. paper)—ISBN 0-7172-5614- 6 (v.6 : alk. paper)—ISBN 0-7172-5615-4 (v.7 : alk. paper)—ISBN 0-7172-5616-2 (v.8 : alk. paper)—ISBN 0-7172-5617-0 (v.9 : alk. paper)—ISBN 0-7172-5618-9 (v.10 : alk. paper)
    1. Science—Study and teaching—Activity programs—Juvenile literature. [1. Science—Experiments. 2. Experiments] I. Grolier Educational (Firm)

LB1585.S335 2002
507.1'2—dc21

                                                      2001040519

ABOUT THIS SET

Science Activities gives children a chance to explore fascinating topics from the world of science using the same methods that professional scientists use to solve problems. This set introduces young scientists to the scientific method by focusing on the importance of planning experiments, conducting them in a rigorous fashion so that a fair test can be carried out, recording all the stages, and organizing and analyzing the data to draw conclusions. Readers will have the chance to conduct exciting and innovative hands-on activities and to learn how to record and analyze their experiments and results in a variety of ways.

Every volume of *Science Activities* contains 10 step-by-step experiments, along with follow-up activities that encourage readers to find out more about the subject. The activities are explained and enhanced with detailed introductory and analysis sections. Colorful photos illustrate each activity, and every book is packed full of pictures and illustrations explaining the details of each topic.

By working fun and educational experiments into the context of the scientific method, anyone using this set can get a feel for how professional scientists go about their work. Most importantly, just have fun!

CONTENTS

VOLUME 10
WEATHER AND CLIMATE

INTRODUCTION

The weather is constantly changing, but our ability to predict the weather is improving all the time. This book will give you the chance to build your own equipment for predicting weather changes.

The weather has an effect on everything we do. We look forward to sunny days and watch out for rainy days, thunderstorms, snow, and blizzards. The weather is vital for growing crops. But, it can also destroy them. Plants need both sunlight and rain, but too much of either can damage plants and reduce the amount of food that we can grow. All living things are adapted to certain weather conditions; and if they change drastically, the organisms might not be able to adapt quick enough to survive.

We notice the weather the most when it is bad. Very bad weather can cause disasters. Floods, hurricanes, typhoons, and droughts all cause serious damage to plants, animals, and people. Tens of thousands of people are caught in severe storms every year. At their worst, storms can cause the loss of crops, homes, and even lives.

For these reasons it is important for us to be able to predict the weather. By studying the atmosphere, clouds, winds, and the various forms of precipitation (water from the air), such as rain, snow, hail, sleet, and fog, scientists can predict when bad weather is on the way. Weather forecasters use monitoring equipment to collect information every

A satellite image of Earth. Satellite technology allows scientists to observe global weather patterns closely.

day, and they use this information to make predictions about the weather. Forecasting weather is different from other branches of science. Weather conditions around the world are constantly changing. So, it is not possible to repeat scientific observations under exactly the same conditions every time. However, general patterns of weather do occur, and it is these patterns that weather forecasters look for and study.

Some of the activities in this book will help you become an amateur weather forecaster. You will have the opportunity to make equipment similar to that used by professional forecasters. After keeping records and charting the weather conditions over a period of time, you should be able to predict the weather using your equipment.

Weather information is usually drawn on weather charts, which show temperature, expected rainfall or snowfall, and areas of high and low pressure. If you measure the weather conditions in different parts of your city or neighborhood, you can draw up a chart of the weather where you live.

Weather patterns are not always fast-moving. A good weather forecaster is thorough and will consider the results of observations made over a period of several weeks before making a forecast. Predicting the weather relies a lot on observation: Keep a log of weather conditions to compare with the results that your new weather-measuring instruments may show you.

One of the most important things to keep in mind when you are observing the weather is to realize how powerful it can be. Some weather conditions can be very dangerous. Only fully trained weather professionals should carry out observations in conditions such as thunderstorms, floods, or tornadoes. The risk of being struck by lightning is small, but even being near a lightning strike can be dangerous. The power of flood waters can carry off trucks and cars. The force of a tornado can destroy whole houses. It is important that if you are unsure about whether you should carry out an experiment because of the possibility of bad weather, you check with an adult before you begin.

🔲 *The monsoon rains that fall at the same time each year provide vital water for crops in India and Southeast Asia, but the monsoon also brings floods.*

The good science guide

Science is not only a collection of facts—it is the process that scientists use to gather information. Follow this good science guide to get the most out of each experiment.

• Carry out each experiment more than once. This prevents accidental mistakes skewing the results. The more times you carry out an experiment, the easier it will be to see if your results are accurate.
• Decide how you will write down your results. You can use a variety of different methods, such as descriptions, diagrams, tables, charts, and graphs. Choose the methods that will make your results easy to read and understand.
• Be sure to write your results down as you are doing the experiment. If one of the results seems very different from the others, it could be because of a problem with the experiment that you should fix immediately.
• Drawing a graph of your results can be very useful because it helps fill in the gaps in your experiment. Imagine, for example, that you plot time along the bottom of the graph and temperature up the side. If you measure the temperature ten times, you can put the results on the graph as dots. Use a ruler to draw a straight line through all the dots. You can now estimate what happened in between each dot, or measurement, by picking any point along the line and reading the time and temperature for that point from the sides of the graph.
• Learn from your mistakes. Some of the most exciting findings in science came from an unexpected result. If your results do not tally with your predictions, try to find out why.
• You should always be careful when carrying out or preparing any experiment, whether it is dangerous or not. Make sure you know the safety rules before you start working.
• Never begin an experiment until you have talked to an adult about what you are going to do.

ACTIVITY 1
EARTH'S ATMOSPHERE

All the water in the world goes around and around in a cycle. When water evaporates from Earth's oceans, it rises and condenses in the atmosphere. That forms clouds, which make rain that keeps the cycle going.

Earth is surrounded by a layer of gases about 600 miles (1,000km) deep. This layer of air is called the atmosphere. There would be no life on Earth without the mixture of gases in this layer. Four-fifths of the atmosphere is nitrogen gas, and most of the rest is oxygen. Animals use this oxygen to breathe. Other gases in the atmosphere include carbon dioxide, which plants need in order to grow, and water vapor.

Earth's atmosphere is divided into a number of different layers. The thermosphere lies between 50 and 310 miles (80 and 500km) above Earth's surface. Beneath it, between 31 and 50 miles (50 and 80km) above Earth, is the mesosphere.

Below the mesosphere is the stratosphere (6 to 31 miles or 10 to 50km). The air at this level is too thin to breathe. It is also very cold. Weather balloons and some aircraft go up to this level.

At about 30 miles (50km) above Earth's surface is a layer rich in ozone gas (a form of oxygen). This important layer helps block out harmful rays from the

A spacecraft flies above clouds in the atmosphere. Clouds form when water evaporates from Earth and rises into the atmosphere, cooling and condensing.

Sun, called ultraviolet radiation. The gases in this layer are still thin, so the Sun's heat passes through them. There is neither water vapor nor clouds at this level.

The layer nearest Earth is called the troposphere, and it is this layer that affects the weather. The troposphere contains three-quarters of the atmosphere. Most of Earth's gases are compressed into this space, which is only between 6 and 10 miles (10 to 16km) thick—from 0 to about 6 miles (10km) above the ground.

HEATING EARTH'S ATMOSPHERE

As Earth orbits the Sun, it also spins. Earth is tilted at a 23.5-degree angle as it spins. It is this tilt that causes the seasons of spring, summer, fall, and winter. When the northern part of Earth, called the

Northern Hemisphere, is tilted toward the Sun, it is summer in the north. The Sun is higher in the sky, and the Sun's rays hit the ground steeply. For this reason more heat reaches Earth. In the winter the rays hit the surface at a shallower angle and spread over a wider area, making the weather colder.

THE WATER CYCLE

The way that the Sun heats Earth affects the amount of rain that falls. The Sun's rays heat the oceans. That causes the water to evaporate (change into a gas called water vapor). Warm air can hold more water vapor than cold air. Air warmed by the Sun takes in or absorbs water vapor. This moist air then rises. As it rises, it cools. The air cannot hold onto the water vapor. Some of the water vapor condenses, changing back from a gas to a liquid, as very small water droplets. These water droplets make up clouds. You can make a model of the water cycle in the activity on the following pages.

The troposphere contains three-quarters of the water vapor in the atmosphere. Nearly all the clouds, rain, and snow occur in this layer.

The mesosphere has the same mixture of oxygen, nitrogen, and carbon dioxide as lower layers, but it has very little water vapor.

Jet planes fly in the stratosphere. The ozone layer is in the upper part of this layer.

Spectacular light effects called auroras can be seen in the thermosphere, the most distant layer of atmosphere.

Earth's atmosphere stretches 600 miles up from the surface. Only the layer of air closest to Earth—the troposphere—affects the weather. The troposphere is where clouds form, and where rain and snow fall from.

The greenhouse effect

Many people are worried about the effect that pollution is having on the balance of gases in the atmosphere. We could be changing the weather and climate irreversibly.

The atmosphere contains small amounts of carbon dioxide gas. When we burn fossil fuels such as oil and coal for motor vehicles, in industry, and to make electricity, we release large quantities of carbon dioxide. Some of this extra gas is absorbed by plants, but much of it drifts up into the atmosphere. Carbon dioxide lets sunlight through but traps heat that rises from the warm Earth. This is called the greenhouse effect, since the carbon dioxide acts like the glass in a greenhouse. The increase in carbon dioxide, and other gases such as methane, is gradually changing Earth's climate. As a result, polar ice sheets and alpine glaciers could melt at a worrying rate. Also, as temperatures rise, water begins to expand slowly. These factors may combine to cause a global rise in sea levels, which could flood low-lying areas over the next few decades.

The Water Cycle

Goals

1. **Make a working model of the water cycle.**
2. **Show how water evaporates, condenses, and then falls to Earth as rain.**

What you will need:

- *large plastic bowl*
- *small container*
- *water*
- *some plastic wrap (cling film)*
- *string or a large rubber band*
- *two balls of modeling clay*

1 Place the small container in the center of the large bowl. Use a blob of modeling clay to fix the small container in place so it doesn't move around when you add water.

2 Pour water into the large bowl around the edge of the small container. Make sure no water goes into the small container.

3 Cover the bowl with plastic wrap. Make sure that it cannot slip by tying it with string or securing it with a rubber band.

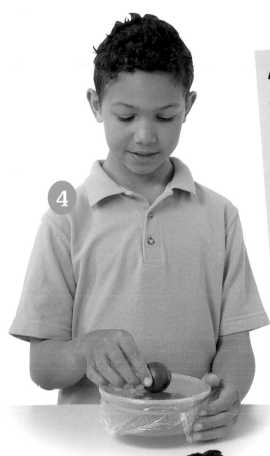

How a raindrop forms

Raindrops form in clouds in Earth's lower atmosphere. As a cloud rises, it cools in the colder air. That turns some of the water vapor that makes up the cloud into tiny droplets of water. The air in the clouds is constantly moving in currents. The currents make the water droplets crash into each other. When they collide, water drops join together. If enough of them cluster into a heavy drop, they fall back to Earth as rain. Sometimes raindrops form around tiny particles of salt, dust, pollen, and volcanic dust from eruptions.

4 Place a ball of modeling clay in the center of the plastic wrap to make the wrap dip over the small container.

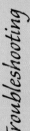

Troubleshooting

What if no water drips into the small container?

If there is no sun, try heating the containers using a lightbulb or a sunlamp. Some places are colder than others, and you may need to repeat the experiment with the bowl placed near a heater. But be careful not to put it too close since you do not want to melt the bowl!

Once you have set up the experiment, do not move the bowl since that could lead to water being spilled and a misleading measurement appearing in your final results.

5 Place the completed experiment in the sun, and watch what happens to the water. Use a thermometer to take the temperature of the water in the small container.

FOLLOW-UP The water cycle

You can use your model of the water cycle to re-create the greenhouse effect. Find a glass cake cover big enough to fit over the bowl.

1 Set up the activity as before. This time, use a stopwatch to time how long it takes for a measured amount of water to evaporate and condense into the small container.

2 Now repeat the activity, and this time place the glass cover over the model. Does the water evaporate more quickly? Take the temperature of the water after each experiment. Is it hotter with or without the glass cover?

3 To re-create the melting ice caps, place chilled water in the bowl with some ice cubes floating in the water. See how long the ice cubes take to melt if the experiment is not under the cake cover. Then repeat the experiment with the cake cover to see if the ice melts faster.

You can compare how the heat of the Sun changes the amount of water that evaporates by taking the temperature where your model of the water cycle is and then measuring the amount of water that collects in the small container. On days when the Sun's rays are less strong and the air is cooler, you should find that less water collects in the small container. Record the temperature of the air, and compare it with the amount of water collected. To make this easier to see, draw the results on a bar chart.

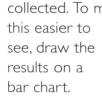

ANALYSIS

Earth's atmosphere

In your model of the water cycle the water that evaporates represents the water vapor that forms clouds. It then condenses back into the small container. Although it is not the same as rainfall, it represents the rain that falls. When rainwater falls on land, it is collected by streams, which run into rivers and then on into the sea. On its route to the sea water gushes across the land, carving deep canyons in the surface of Earth over thousands of years. Waterfalls occur where water plunges down from an area of hard rock to an area of softer rock that has been worn away over time. During its journey water in the atmosphere returns to the sea, where it evaporated from and will evaporate again, returning to the atmosphere over and over in a cycle.

The glass cake cover over your follow-up experiment represents high levels of carbon

Water falls to Earth as rain, snow, and hail. The water then runs across the land, down to the sea. Some water gushes down waterfalls on its journey.

Fear of floods

If the temperature rises only a few degrees more, it could lead to the ice caps over the North and South Poles melting. The water released from the ice caps would flood low-lying land throughout the world. Cities such as New York, London, and Sydney (shown above) could even be at risk.

dioxide in the atmosphere. Like the panes of glass in a greenhouse, your glass cover transmits sunlight but prevents heat from escaping. So the temperature of the water in the small container should be higher in your greenhouse than in the main activity, which represents an unpolluted water cycle. When you step inside a greenhouse, you can feel that it is warmer inside than outside. The ice cubes will melt more quickly when the glass cover is in place. While we need greenhouse gases in the atmosphere to keep Earth warm enough to live on, a buildup of gases can cause climate changes and floods.

ACTIVITY 2
WATER IN THE AIR

You can't always see the water in the air, but you can feel it. Sometimes your skin feels sticky on hot days. That is because your sweat cannot evaporate—there is too much water vapor floating in the air around you.

A bank of fog fills a river valley, causing visibility problems for drivers on the lower roads.

More than 90 percent of the water on Earth is in the oceans and rivers, in the ground, and frozen as ice. The rest is in the air. Most of this water is in the form of gas (water vapor), but it also forms clouds, rain, snow, and hail. The amount of water vapor in the air is called the humidity. The warmer the air is, the more water vapor it can hold.

The amount of moisture in the air is often described as the "relative humidity." It is measured using an instrument called a hygrometer—you can make one in the activity on the following pages. Relative humidity is a measure of how much water the air is holding at a given temperature, compared to the maximum water the air could hold at that temperature. If the air temperature is 80 °F (27°C) and the relative humidity is 50 percent, then it is holding 50 percent of the water it can hold at 80 °F (27°C).

For clouds to form and rain to fall, the air has to have 100 percent relative humidity. This measurement only applies to the place in which clouds are forming or rain is falling. For example, rain will fall from clouds where the humidity is 100 percent, but beneath the clouds the relative humidity will be lower. The rain itself will be falling into an area where humidity is less than 100 percent.

The presence of moisture in the air creates different types of weather, such as fog, in which visibility is less than 0.6 miles (1km), and mist, in which visibility is between 0.6 and 1.25 miles (1 and 2km). Fog and mist form near the ground when water vapor changes into tiny water drops. These droplets remain suspended in the air. The main difference between clouds and fog or mist is that clouds form when moist air rises and then cools, but fog and mist form when air cools near the ground. Fog and mist often happen at night. They are more common in wet areas, such as near rivers or lakes, or in mountain regions, where the air is cold and heavy and sinks down into valleys.

Fog and mist normally appear when the weather is fair and calm. The air has to be saturated with water vapor for them to form. One of the thickest types of fog is called advection fog (see box). Advection is the name given to air that moves horizontally across the ground. Advection fog forms because heavier, humid air near the ground does not mix with drier air above it. Sunlight causes the fog to evaporate or burn off, but sometimes the fog is so thick that sunlight cannot get through and the fog remains for a number of days. Mists usually burn off much more quickly.

Fog formation

Advection fogs form when warm, moist air moves across cooler water or land. They are more common in winter and early spring, when snow starts to melt. Radiation fog forms at night. As the temperatures drop, fog forms in the cool areas near the ground and rises.

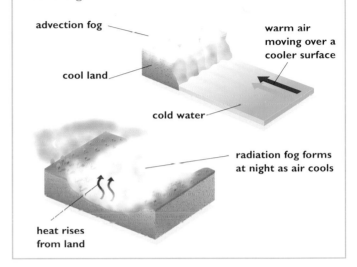

advection fog

warm air moving over a cooler surface

cool land

cold water

radiation fog forms at night as air cools

heat rises from land

Dew point

Dew and frost are both also caused by water in the air. Dew is a layer of water that settles on the ground, or other surfaces, in the early morning. It is caused by the condensation (changing to liquid) of water vapor in the air. At night the temperature cools, especially on nights when there are no clouds to keep in Earth's heat. Eventually the air reaches a temperature that is too cool to hold the water vapor. It is called the dew point. As soon as the dew point is reached, the excess water in the air condenses. If the dew point is below 32 °F (0 °C), the water vapor forms ice crystals, which cover everything with frost.

The dew-point temperature gives a much better estimate of the amount of moisture actually present in the air than relative humidity. The higher the dew-point temperature, the more moisture there is in the air.

You can easily find the dew point yourself. Fill a can half-full with room-temperature water. Place a thermometer in the water, and stir in some ice, a little bit at a time. Do this slowly so you can watch the temperature on the thermometer fall. Water will start to condense on the outside of your can. The temperature at which this happens is the dew-point temperature.

Making a Hygrometer

ACTIVITY

Goals

1. Make a hygrometer.
2. Use a hygrometer to measure the amount of humidity in the air.

What you will need:

- a board
- pen
- two thermometers
- glue
- bottle cap from a soft drink bottle
- muslin or cheesecloth
- water
- tape
- ruler

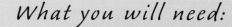

1 Draw evenly spaced lines across the board.

2 Tape the two thermometers, side by side and level with each other, onto the board. Leave enough space between them so that you can read them easily.

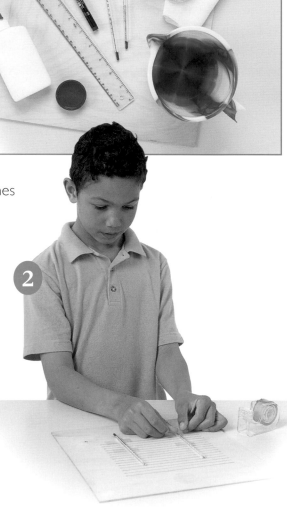

3 Glue the bottle cap about 1 inch (2.5cm) below one of the thermometers.

4 Prop up the board. Cut a small piece of muslin or cheesecloth, and dip it in water to wet it.

Adapting to humidity

We normally keep cool by sweating. When the sweat evaporates from our skin, it takes heat with it—cooling us off. In very humid air sweat does not evaporate off our bodies to keep us cool. For this reason hard physical labor in humid air can be exhausting if we are not used to it. But with practice our bodies can adapt to humid conditions.

5 Place the wet cloth into the bottle cap, and wrap the cloth around the bottom of the thermometer. Fill the cap with water. Wait about 30 minutes, and then record the temperatures on the two thermometers. The lines on the board are there to make it easier for you to read the thermometers.

6 Place the board outside, wait 30 minutes, and read the temperatures again. Where was the bigger difference in temperatures?

FOLLOW-UP Making a hygrometer

To find out how the humidity affects the weather, put together a chart that shows the relative humidity for each day. Record the type of weather that you have each day. What sort of pattern do you notice?

Knowing the humidity of the air outside will help you predict the weather, but the air in each room of your house will also have a different humidity. Place your hygrometer in different rooms in the house, and record the temperatures. Which room do you think might have the highest humidity—think about how water boils and rises into the air as water vapor.

▶ *You can test your hygrometer inside. Place it in the bathroom after someone has had a bath or shower, or ask an adult to keep it in the kitchen while they are cooking.*

A hair hygrometer

Some of the earliest hygrometers used hair to measure the humidity in the air. Hair becomes longer with higher relative humidity and shorter with lower relative humidity. The hair in a hygrometer is attached to a lever that magnifies the small change in hair length to give an estimate of the humidity. You can make a simple hair hygrometer of your own.

You will need:
a long hair
a board or piece of
  cardboard
two thumbtacks
tape
straw
pen

First, tack the straw onto the board. Make sure the straw is loose enough to spin freely on the board. Wet the hair, and tape one end of it to the straw. Place the second thumbtack on the board below the straw. Wind the other end of the hair around the tack until it is straight and taught. The straw should be pointing toward the bottom of the board (see below).

Draw a curve on the board as shown below. Label the bottom of the curve "Humid" and the top of the curve "Dry." As the hair shrinks and lengthens, it will move the straw and alert you to the amount of humidity in the air.

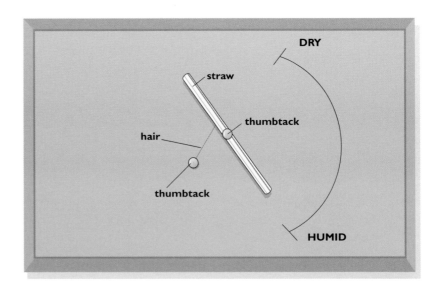

ANALYSIS

Water in the air

When water evaporates, it takes heat energy from its surroundings. In this activity, when water evaporated from the wet cloth, it took heat energy from the thermometer. For this reason the temperature of the "wet bulb" thermometer (the one wrapped in the wet cloth) should have always been lower than the temperature on the "dry bulb" thermometer.

As you may have noticed in the activity and in the follow-ups, when the air is dry, a lot of water evaporates from the muslin, producing a lower temperature on the wet bulb thermometer. If the air is humid, less water will evaporate from the cloth, producing a higher temperature on the wet bulb thermometer. The more humid the air, the greater the difference in temperatures between the two thermometers.

You can also use your hygrometer to measure the relative humidity. Using the chart below, you can find out the percentage of relative humidity in the air. Check the accuracy of your hygrometer by looking in the newspaper or on the Internet to compare your readings with those of the National Weather Service.

Relative humidity chart

You can use this chart to find the relative humidity. Simply find the dry bulb reading in the top row (green numbers) and the wet bulb reading in the column on the far left (red numbers). The place where the row and the column intersect shows the percentage of relative humidity (blue numbers) in the air.

dry bulb reading in °F (in green)

wet bulb reading in °F (in red)	70	71	72	73	74	75	76	77
55	36	33	31	29	26	24	22	20
56	40	37	34	32	29	27	25	23
57	44	41	38	35	33	30	28	26
58	48	45	42	39	36	34	31	29
59	51	48	45	42	39	37	34	32
60	55	52	49	46	43	40	38	35
61	59	56	53	50	47	44	41	39
62	64	60	57	53	50	47	44	42
63	68	64	61	57	54	51	48	45
64	72	68	65	61	58	54	51	48
65	77	72	69	65	61	58	55	52
66	81	77	73	69	65	62	59	56
67	86	81	77	73	69	66	62	59
68	90	86	82	78	74	70	66	63
69	95	90	86	82	78	74	70	67
70	100	95	91	86	82	78	74	71
71		100	95	91	86	82	78	74
72			100	95	91	86	82	79
73				100	95	91	87	83
74					100	95	91	87
75						100	96	91
76							100	96
77								100

ACTIVITY 3
CLOUDS

Our planet's atmosphere contains only a small amount of water vapor, in the layer closest to Earth. That is where clouds—a mixture of water droplets, water vapor, and ice crystals—are made.

Clouds start off when water evaporates from the oceans or the ground and clusters around tiny dirt or salt particles floating in the air to make water droplets. Water molecules are so small that it takes about a million to make one raindrop. The droplets have to become larger before they can fall as rain or snow. Droplets grow as water molecules join, or when they bump into each other and link. As the vapor rises, it cools, and the water condenses or freezes. A cloud can consist of water vapor, water droplets, ice crystals, or any mixture of all three, depending on the temperature of the cloud.

Winds carry clouds into areas of warmer or cooler air. If a new cloud moves into an area of warm air, some of the water droplets turn back into water vapor, and the cloud gets smaller. If the cloud is cooled, more water droplets form, and the cloud gets

We can see clouds because they are made of water droplets, water vapor, and ice crystals that reflect and scatter sunlight.

bigger. When the cloud moves over land, it is forced upward and cools very rapidly, which creates raindrops that fall back to Earth. That is one of the reasons why mountains near coastal areas often have very heavy rainfall. One side of the mountain will usually be dry because the clouds become warmer after they pass over the top of the mountain, and water droplets turn back into water vapor. The clouds then get smaller, and the rain stops. This dry, back slope of a mountain is called the rain shadow.

The shape of clouds can give clues as to what type of weather we can expect. Types of clouds were first named by an English chemist, Luke Howard

(1772–1864), in 1802. The names he gave them come from Latin words and describe the way the clouds look. The three main types of cloud named by Howard are *cumulus*, meaning "heap," *stratus*, meaning "layer," and *cirrus*, which means "curl of hair."

Cumulus clouds are large and look like cotton wool. They are made of tiny water droplets, which form as warm rising air condenses in the cool upper atmosphere. Small cumulus clouds are a sign that the weather will be nice. Larger swelling or towering cumulus clouds normally bring rain with them. Large black clouds in the sky are called cumulonimbus. They are storm clouds and are a good sign that a thunderstorm is due soon.

■ *This type of lenticular (lens-shaped) cloud formation is sometimes mistaken for one or more UFOs.*

Higher in the sky are stratus clouds. They often yield continual heavy rain or drizzle. They are usually only 3,300 feet (1km) thick but can be anything up to 600 miles (1,000km) wide. They form when a layer of warm, moist air flows under or over a mass of cold air. Stratus clouds rarely reach more than $\frac{1}{4}$ mile (500m) above the ground. Altostratus clouds are usually higher in the sky, between 2 miles ($3\frac{1}{4}$km) and 7 miles ($11\frac{1}{4}$km) above ground level. However, the highest clouds in the sky are cirrus clouds, wispy clouds that form between 5 miles (8 km) and 8 miles (13 km) above the ground. Clouds generally form at lower altitudes in polar regions and higher over the tropics.

Types of clouds

Different cloud shapes, sizes, and colors can tell you what sort of weather to expect. Dark cumulus clouds (1) are a sign that rain may fall. Stratus clouds (2) are gray, low-lying clouds that produce drizzle and snow when it is cold enough.

Altocumulus clouds (3) are white clouds that generally form in regular shapes and sometimes signal a thunderstorm. Cirrus clouds (4), sometimes called mares' tails, are very light and wispy, they are a sign of good weather.

Making Clouds

Goals

1. **Show that clouds are formed by water vapor.**
2. **Re-create the way that clouds form.**

What you will need:

- *jar*
- *warm water*
- *funnel*
- *ice cubes*
- *stopwatch or watch with second hand*

1 Fill the jar with hot water from the hot water tap.

2 Place the funnel in the neck of the jar.

Safety tip

The water needs to be very hot for this activity to work. Make sure you have an adult present when using hot water.

3 Fill the funnel with the ice cubes.

3

Troubleshooting

What if I can't see any clouds forming?

If you have trouble seeing the clouds forming, you may need to use hotter water. Ask an adult to boil some water for you and pour it into the jar. Do not touch the jar until the hot water has cooled down, and use oven mitts for safety.

4 Watch for clouds to form over the funnel. Time how long it takes for the clouds to form. Place a sheet of dark paper behind the jar to make it easier to see the clouds.

4

Dry ice

Theaters, film, and music videos use a process similar to this experiment to make clouds and mist on stage. The main difference is that they use frozen carbon dioxide, called dry ice. Dry ice freezes at a temperature of −110.2 °F (−79 °C). That is cold enough to burn your hands. When dry ice is placed in a kettle with boiling water or in a dry ice machine, the carbon dioxide changes very rapidly back into a gas. This gas, mixed with the water vapor, is released through a hose at the front of the dry ice machine to produce clouds.

FOLLOW-UP Making clouds

You can repeat this activity using different temperatures of water and timing how quickly the clouds form. Do the clouds form faster or slower with cooler water? You can compare your findings by plotting a graph of the temperature against the time it took the ice to turn into a cloud.

Try the experiment again using different amounts of ice. Time how long it takes for different amounts to form clouds. When you use less ice, does the cloud take less time to appear?

You can also set up a cloud watch in your area. Record the different types of clouds that you see in the sky over a period of time. Draw pictures (below) or take photographs of the clouds you see, and try to figure out what type they are. You should also record the weather conditions for that day and the next day. Do certain types of clouds come before certain types of weather? Are certain types of clouds more common during certain times of the year? Use the information that you gather to try and predict the weather. Check the weather reports in your area to see if your predictions were correct.

▉ *Different types of clouds usually bring with them different types of weather. By watching the clouds, you can try to predict the weather.*

ANALYSIS

Clouds

In this experiment you saw clouds forming above the funnel because of the difference in temperature between the air above the hot water and the air above the ice. As the hot water in the jar evaporated, water vapor formed in the jar. The warm water vapor is less dense than the air around it, so it rose through the jar and the funnel until it encountered cooler air above the ice. As the water vapor came into contact with this cooler air, it condensed (turned back into a liquid) and formed a cloud.

You should have noticed that the clouds that formed above your jar were not very thick, dark, or billowing. In fact, they should have been very thin and wispy. That is because there was not a lot of water vapor in the air, and also because there were probably not too many dust particles, or pollution particles, in the air above the jar for the droplets to form around.

In the follow-up you should have noticed that the cooler the water is, the fewer the clouds that form. That is because cool water does not give off as much water vapor as hot water, so there is less water in the air to condense and form clouds. Similarly, if you use fewer ice cubes, the air above the funnel will be warmer, and less of the water vapor will condense to form clouds.

Rain shadow

Sometimes one area of land can get a lot of rain or snow (precipitation), while just a few miles away there is almost no precipitation, and the land is very dry. This happens when the two areas of land are separated by a mountain range. The dry area lies in a rain shadow. Rain shadows occur on the leeward (sheltered) sides of mountains.

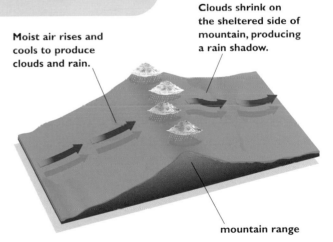

Moist air rises and cools to produce clouds and rain.

Clouds shrink on the sheltered side of mountain, producing a rain shadow.

mountain range

On the windward (windy) side of the mountain moist air rises and cools, forming clouds that produce heavy rainfall. As the air falls down the leeward side, it warms up. The water droplets turn back into water vapor, the clouds get smaller, and the rain stops.

◀ **The desert to the east of the Sierra Nevada mountain range (left) is in a rain shadow. But plenty of rain falls to the west of the mountain range.**

ACTIVITY 4
SNOW, HAIL, AND ICE

Snow, hail, and ice are different types of precipitation that form in clouds from water vapor and eventually fall to the ground. The particular type that develops depends on the surrounding temperature and air currents.

Snowy slopes make great playgrounds for everyone. The snow flakes will settle on the ground as long as the temperature is below 32 °F (0 °C).

Anything that falls from a cloud, such as rain, snow, hail, sleet, or drizzle, is a type of precipitation (moisture). Each type starts off as microscopic water droplets, but they each form in slightly different ways. Snow forms when tiny droplets of water freeze to make ice crystals. The crystals then grow to make more complex shapes as more crystals freeze onto them. These shapes are snowflakes. Snowflakes always have six sides. The crystals can form an infinite number of different shapes, but every crystal has six sides. Naturalist Wilson Bentley spent 40 years studying snowflakes and never found two with identical patterns.

As the flakes of snow get heavier, they fall because of the effects of gravity. As long as the temperature on the ground is below 32 °F (0 °C), the flakes will remain frozen and cover the ground with a layer of snow.

Skiers prefer light, powdery snow, which usually forms at temperatures below 20 °F (-7 °C). If there is no wind to pack the snow together, then it becomes very fluffy. Avalanches are large masses of snow, ice, or rock that slide rapidly down a mountain slope. They happen because the amount of snow that has fallen is too heavy for the slope it is lying on, and it cannot stay in place any longer. Avalanches can be triggered by vibrations or loud noises. They are very destructive. Thousands of tons of snow can travel at 100 miles an hour (160km/h), flattening everything in their path.

Inside dark, heavy storm clouds, called cumulonimbus clouds, air currents are constantly rising and falling. These clouds contain water droplets, ice crystals, large raindrops, snowflakes, and hailstones. The water droplets are carried high up in the cloud, where they freeze and then fall again. However, instead of falling to Earth, the frozen droplets are swept back up. Each time they go back up they pass above the freezing level, and another layer of ice is added to the frozen raindrop. Eventually the ball of ice is so heavy that the wind inside the cloud cannot keep it inside any more, and the lump of ice falls to Earth as a hailstone.

Pancake ice forms when slushy snow on the top of a lake freezes. The ice clusters into floating disks like these on Lake Superior, which are also covered with hail.

Cloud seeding

Cloud seeding is the method of adding chemicals to a cloud to produce liquid precipitation. Seeding relies on clouds that contain supercooled water—water whose temperature is colder than 32 °F (0 °C). Planes spray a chemical, silver iodide, into the clouds. The silver iodide has a crystal structure similar to ice and will cause the supercooled water to suddenly crystalize (form ice). The heavy ice particles fall and melt at lower altitudes to form rain.

plane sprays drops of silver iodide

ice

water droplets

rising water vapor

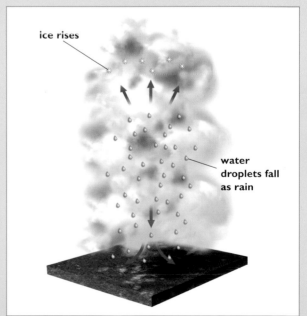

ice rises

water droplets fall as rain

Making Hailstones

Goals

1. **Reproduce the way that hailstones form.**
2. **Examine the separate layers that form inside the hailstone.**

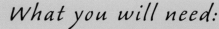

What you will need:

- *three or four different-sized flexible containers*
- *water*
- *freezer*
- *food dyes (at least 2 different colors)*
- *refrigerator*
- *cloth*
- *hammer*
- *tray*
- *measuring cup*

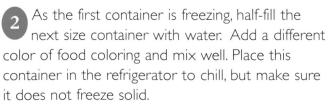

1 Put some water in the measuring cup, and use one of the dyes to color it. Pour water into the smallest container you are using. Place the container in the freezer until it is frozen.

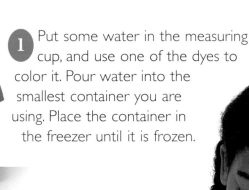

2 As the first container is freezing, half-fill the next size container with water. Add a different color of food coloring and mix well. Place this container in the refrigerator to chill, but make sure it does not freeze solid.

3 Turn the ice out of the first container, and drop it into the second container, with the chilled water. Place this in the freezer, and leave it until the water is frozen solid.

4 Repeat steps 2 and 3 until you have used all the containers. Make sure you use a different color of food dye in each container. If you have just two colors, you can alternate between the two colors.

5 Place the cloth on the tray. When the water in the last container is frozen solid, turn out your hailstone onto the cloth. Cover it with the end of the cloth.

Giant hailstones

The largest hailstone reported in the United States fell in Coffeyville, Kansas, in September 1970. This massive hailstone measured 17.5 inches across, and weighed 1.67 pounds.

6 Gently tap the hailstone with the hammer to break it open (have an adult present for this part). It should break open to reveal the separate layers.

FOLLOW-UP

Making hailstones

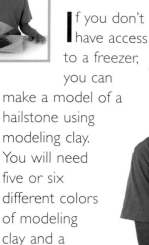

If you don't have access to a freezer, you can make a model of a hailstone using modeling clay. You will need five or six different colors of modeling clay and a thread. First, make a small ball of clay.

Using a different color of clay, surround the first ball with this new color (left). Continue making layers with different colors of clay (or alternate colors) until you have a large ball. Use a length of thread to cut the clay hailstone cleanly in half (top right) and reveal the layers (bottom right).

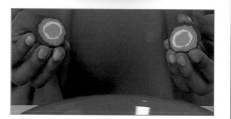

ANALYSIS

Snow, hail, and ice

In this activity you built up a hailstone using layers of frozen water, similar to how hailstones are formed in clouds.

Some of the largest hailstones ever measured were about the size of a grapefruit. Hailstones much smaller than this can flatten fields of crops and destroy fruit. In areas where hail falls regularly, food production can be difficult. In the past engineers in Russia would fire rockets into thunderclouds to try to make hailstones smaller. Each rocket contained silver iodide, which helped turn the freezing hailstones into rain (see box, page 25).

Freezing raindrops are a similar type of weather event. Frozen raindrops occur when raindrops form at high levels and fall through a shallow layer of cold air just above ground level. They freeze and arrive on the ground as a wet kind of snow called sleet. Sleet collects as round particles of ice. Some weather forecast-ers call a combination of snow and sleet "sneet." If it is mixed with very fine rain or drizzle, then it is called "snizzle." These types of precipitation often fall in the northern United States just before a major snowfall.

If snow falls in very windy conditions, with winds more than 35 miles per hour (55km/h), it is called a blizzard. The word blizzard comes from the German word *blitzartig*, meaning "lightninglike." Blizzards often feel colder than ordinary snowstorms because of the strong winds that accompany them. This effect is called wind-chill factor.

The wind-chill factor is a measure of how quickly a person loses body heat due to the wind. For example, at 38 °F in a 30 miles per hour wind, the wind-chill is 10 °F. So someone caught in such weather would cool down as if the temperature was only 10 °F, even though water would not freeze in these conditions.

ACTIVITY 5
RAIN AND FLOODS

When areas receive too much precipitation in the form of rain or melting snow, they may flood. When they receive too little, they may experience a very dry period called a drought. Both conditions bring many problems.

The flood barrier across the Thames River, London, keeps the water levels from rising too high.

Water that seeps into the ground sinks down until it reaches solid rock, beyond which it cannot travel. Generally, for some distance above the solid rock, the ground is saturated with water—it has soaked up all the water it can. The upper point at which the saturation ends is called the water table. When more water seeps into the ground, the water table rises. When the water rises to ground level, the ground is fully saturated and excess water flows across the ground as surface runoff. If the surface runoff reaches a river, the river can quickly rise and might overflow its banks.

Floods occur when there is more water than the ground can hold. Floods can kill people and animals and destroy crops, leading to famine. The force of floodwaters can carry off people, cars, and houses. Many of the people who are killed in floods die when their cars or other vehicles are carried off by the force of the water. Most rivers normally move at about 4 miles per hour (6km/h), with a force of about 66 pounds per square foot. If the water speed is doubled to 8 miles per hour (12km/h), which often happens in floods, then the force of the water is almost four times as strong—enough to easily push a car off a flooded road.

When water seeps slowly down into the ground, it is called infiltration. Water that flows across the ground is called surface runoff. Floods happen when excess water has nowhere to go.

In some places the water table is right on the surface. Water fills these places until the water level is the same as the water table level, making rivers and lakes. A flat expanse of ground near a river is called a flood plain. They are the most flood-prone areas, since the water that overflows the river's banks cannot seep into the ground of the flood plain and will instead move across it.

In the activity on the following pages you will make a model of a flood to see what happens with different ground types and different surfaces.

Making a Flood

Goals

1. **Make a model to demonstrate why flood plains flood.**
2. **Use rocks and sponges to illustrate what ground types are most likely to flood.**

What you will need:

- *large bowl*
- *large tray*
- *some sponges*
- *measuring cup*
- *water (lots of it)*
- *watering can*
- *freezer*
- *some rocks*

1 Place the bowl in the center of the tray. Place pieces of sponge around the edge of the bowl. The sponges should be dry.

2 Using the cup, fill the bowl with water.

3 Fill the watering can with water. Record the amount of water you put into the can. Start to pour water onto the bowl and the sponges. This is the rain.

What if the water overflows onto the floor?

This experiment may get messy, so find somewhere to do it where it doesn't matter if the floor gets wet. Put the wet sponges on a tray in the freezer to make sure they don't stick to the freezer itself.

If you want to see the effects of a heavier rainstorm, use a hose instead of the watering can. If you use a hose, make sure you only use it outside, and always ask an adult's permission.

4 Keep filling the watering can and raining on the model until the bowl starts to overflow and you can see water on top of the sponges. Record the total amount of water it takes to cause this flooding.

5 Take the still-wet sponges, and put them on a tray in the freezer. Repeat the experiment with the frozen sponges. How much water does it take to cause a flood with frozen "ground"?

6 Repeat the experiment using rocks instead of sponges. How much water does it take to flood rocky "ground"?

FOLLOW-UP

Making a flood

After you have experimented with spongy, frozen, and rocky floodplains, you can also repeat the activity with a sandy floodplain. Simply cover the tray with a layer of dry beach sand (right). You might also want to repeat the activity using wet and dry soil from your yard (be sure to ask permission before digging up any soil).

You can make a small stream by replacing the bowl with a piece of gutter, or a plastic bottle cut in half (ask an adult to cut the bottle in half with a pair of scissors). Use a hose to run water slowly down the gutter or bottle. Instead of a watering can, use a second hose to flood the model. Have the water run first at a trickle, then as a flood, and note the different effects on the sand or soil in your tray. Only try this activity outside in a grassy or sandy area.

ANALYSIS

Rain and floods

When rain falls, the level of water in rivers, lakes, and reservoirs rises. Reservoirs are large artificial basins created for holding water from rainfall or other sources. The water in them is used to irrigate or water crops and for drinking water. Normally the rain that falls will only bring the water levels of rivers, lakes, and reservoirs up to the edge of the banks or basins. However, if more rain than usual falls, they could burst their banks, and the water will flow across the nearby land.

The bowl in the experiment represents a reservoir that overfills as the rain falls and floods the surrounding land. This flooding is caused by surface runoff. There are a number of reasons why flooding can happen when surface runoff occurs. The sponges and rocks surrounding the bowl show some of the conditions that can cause flooding.

The dry sponges represent dry ground that is not yet saturated with water. As the rain falls, this ground becomes saturated. If the soil becomes oversaturated with water, the excess water has to go somewhere. The saturated soil does not cause the flooding—it is the extra water that joins the water already there.

The frozen sponges represent frozen ground. Frozen ground cannot soak up as much water as unfrozen soil. If rain falls, or a layer of snow starts to melt on the surface of this frozen ground, the water cannot soak through.

The rocks represent ground that has gone through a drought, when there is no rainfall to provide water for growing crops. In some parts of the world droughts occur every year. These annual droughts are expected in areas with what is called a savanna climate. This type of climate is found in areas between deserts and

Forceful floods

Many people are tempted to drive through a flood, but that is actually very dangerous. The force of the floodwater can easily sweep a car from the road.

Water 1 foot (30cm) deep can exert a sideways push (lateral force) of 500 pounds (227kg). That is enough to cause a car to slide uncontrollably.

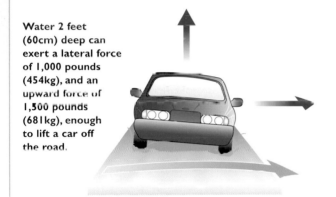

Water 2 feet (60cm) deep can exert a lateral force of 1,000 pounds (454kg), and an upward force of 1,500 pounds (681kg), enough to lift a car off the road.

Muddy water can hide a washed out road, causing a car to drop suddenly into unexpectedly deep water.

If you performed the follow-up activity with the hose and gutter, you would have noticed that the increased volume of water has a huge effect on how fast the tray floods. This is similar to what happens during a monsoon.

Monsoons are very heavy, warm rains that occur in certain parts of the world. In these places the months before the monsoons are hot and dry, and the ground often bakes hard. This is followed by a period of very heavy rains, the monsoon season. The monsoon is important in these areas because the rains are a major source of fresh water for crops. But if the rains start later than expected, or are heavier than expected, severe flooding can result. Crops can be ruined, and people's homes carried away.

The southwest United States is another place prone to flash floods. In this hot, dry region the Sun bakes the ground until it is very hard and dry. When there is a sudden summer thunderstorm, the heavy rain cannot sink into the ground and instead flows over the ground and creates a flash flood. This area contains many canyons, which are the remains of dried-up river beds. Flash floods rush through these canyons at great speed and with great force.

🔲 *The flood plain of a river in Kakadu National Park, Australia. When the river floods, this large, flat area of land can quickly become awash with floodwaters.*

rain forests. Little water falls on the land during a drought, and it becomes baked hard in the sun. Droughts can lead to crop failure and no food for people to eat. Water holes and rivers also dry up. Droughts in poorer countries often lead to famines, and people starve. There can then also be problems with floods. When the rain finally does fall, the ground is so hard that the water cannot soak through the surface, and it remains there, leading to widespread flooding and more destruction.

ACTIVITY 6
THUNDER AND LIGHTNING

Lightning is a powerful electrical discharge that takes place between storm clouds or between the clouds and Earth's surface. Thunder is the sound shock wave caused by the lightning heating and expanding the surrounding air.

One of the most exciting weather phenomena to watch is a thunderstorm, in which lightning hits the ground and thunder makes a terrific noise. The chances of being hit by lightning are very small, but every year people are killed either by a direct hit from a lightning strike or by standing near an object that falls when it is struck by lightning. In the United States about 100 people a year are killed by lightning. Lightning also starts hundreds of forest fires every year.

Lightning is a giant electrical spark that flashes for about one-fifth of a second. Scientists have developed many different theories about how lightning forms. According to one theory, moving air in a storm cloud causes water drops and ice particles to collide and become charged with static

Lightning is a discharge of static electricity in the sky. The two main types of lightning are called streaked, or forked, lightning (above) and sheet lightning.

electricity. The positive electrically charged particles float near the top of the cloud, and the larger, negatively charged particles stay near the bottom. These separated charges become very unstable. They want to be together. For this reason the negative charge jumps toward the nearest positive charge. This could be the top of the cloud, or it could be the ground, which is also positively charged. Different types of lightning take place in different places. Streaked or forked lightning is seen as bright, jagged lines against the sky. Sheet lightning is a large flash that seems to fill the whole sky.

Streaked lightning occurs when the electric spark jumps from the cloud to the ground. Sheet lightning happens from the top to the bottom of a cloud. Lightning consists of a number of different discharges traveling forward and backward. First, a negative charge, called a leader stroke, jumps toward a positive charge. A return stroke then travels back up the same path, giving off the heat that creates the thunder we can hear.

When lightning is released or discharged from a cloud, it creates a lot of heat. The temperature of the electrical discharge is almost 11,000 °F (20,000 °C), making the air expand suddenly and creating a loud noise that we call thunder. Light travels at a speed of 186,000 miles per second (300,000 km/s), while sound travels a lot slower, at a speed of 1,070 feet per second (330m/s). You will always see the lightning before you hear the thunder. If you can count five seconds between the lightning flash and the thunder, then the storm is one mile away (1.6km).

Lightning is attracted to pointed pieces of metal. For this reason many tall buildings have a spike of metal on top called a lightning conductor, connected by a wire to the ground. The wire helps move the lightning away from the building and reduces the risk of damage. In the activity on the following pages you can create an artificial lightning strike using static electricity.

■ *A powerful strike of lightning has left its mark on this tree.*

Electrical discharge

Lightning develops when warm, moist air rises to form storm clouds in which a process called charge separation takes place. Water droplets and ice rub together and become charged with static electricity. Negatively charged particles collect at the base of the clouds, making the tops of the clouds and Earth's surface positively charged. A rush of current—the leader stroke—occurs between the clouds and the ground. When the electrons meet the positive charge, a strong electric current—the return stroke—carries the positive charge up to the clouds.

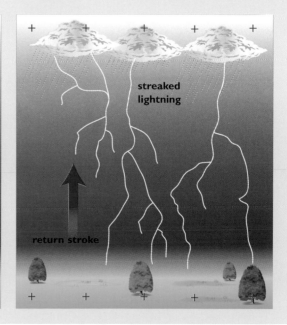

leader stroke

Friction between water drops causes charge separation.

streaked lightning

return stroke

Making Lightning

Goals

1. **Reproduce the circumstances in which lightning comes down to Earth.**
2. **Make an artificial lightning strike.**

What you will need:

- plastic sheet
- adhesive tape
- rubber gloves
- large iron or steel pot (not aluminum) with a plastic handle
- iron or steel fork
- plastic ruler

1 Tape the plastic sheet to a table top.

2 Put on the rubber gloves.

Benjamin Franklin

In the 18th century the American scientist Benjamin Franklin began a series of experiments with electricity. In one he flew a silk kite in a thunderstorm. The kite carried a metal rod and was attached to a long piece of twine tied to a key. Also tied to the key was a piece of silk that Franklin held under a roof so that it remained dry. During the storm Franklin was able to draw a spark from the key to his knuckle and to charge a Leyden jar with electricity from the kite. Several people tried to repeat Franklin's experiment and were killed by electrocution. Franklin was lucky not to have been harmed himself. You should NEVER fly a kite during a thunderstorm.

3 Hold the large pot by its handle. Rub it vigorously on the plastic sheet

Troubleshooting

What if I can't see the spark?
The spark of static electricity that you make this way is only very small. You will be able to see it better if you draw the curtains or carry out the activity in a darkened room.

Safety tip

You must wear rubber gloves because the pan will keep the charge. Try to use a pot with an insulating handle.

4 Take the fork in your other hand, and slowly bring its prongs near the base of the pot. When the gap between the pot and the fork is small, a tiny spark of static electricity should jump across.

5 Repeat the experiment, this time using a plastic ruler.

FOLLOW-UP

Making lightning

After you have tested the fork, you can try making a spark with other materials, such as tin foil (below) and a second pot. You could also carry out the experiment in reverse, by rubbing the fork on the plastic and touching it to the pot. Is there any difference in the size of the spark?

Does the amount of rubbing on the plastic sheet affect the size of the spark and the distance that it jumps to the fork? You can test this by counting the number of times you rub the pot and comparing the size of the sparks created.

ANALYSIS

Thunder and lightning

As the pot is rubbed backward and forward across the plastic sheet, it becomes charged with static electricity. This static electricity is released when a grounding device, such as the steel fork, is brought near. Certain items conduct electricity better than others, and strokes of lightning are attracted to these conductors before striking other items. Lightning conductors are always made of metal. They take the lightning away from buildings and keep it from damaging them.

Rain often helps firefighters put out fires in forests and other areas of land. However, some thunderstorms are not helpful in fighting fires and can actually start them. These storms happen mainly in the western United States and are called dry thunderstorms. The humidity (moisture level in air) in this area is often so low that when rain falls during a thunderstorm, it evaporates (turns to gas) before it reaches the ground. This evaporating rain is called virga. The storms are often very high up above the

ground, with a large layer of very dry air between the bottom of the cloud and the ground. This dry air helps the virga evaporate.

Even though the rain does not make it to the ground, lightning from the clouds can reach the ground. If the forests and woods are dry,

Tall stories

In the animal world giraffes are struck by lightning more than any other because they are so tall. Giraffes move around in groups, which can also increase their chances of being struck. They are not the only animals at risk. In the year 2000 seven elephants were killed in one strike in the Kruger National Park, South Africa. Four-legged animals can also be killed by lightning that strikes nearby. If a four-legged animal is standing near ground that is struck by lightning, then the electricity will spread through the ground and through each of its four feet. This electric shock can stop the animal's heart and kill it.

🔖 *Most forest fires in the United States are started by lightning storms. The destruction is only temporary— new plants soon begin to grow through the ashes.*

then the lightning can start fires. The fact that no rain falls means that there is no natural help to put out the fire. About 75,000 forest fires are started each year in the United States through lightning strikes.

Lightning often strikes the same place more than once. The Empire State Building in New York City, for example, is struck by lightning around 500 times each year.

The safest place to be during a lightning strike is inside a car. That is because the electricity passes through the car's metal body and jumps safely to the ground. One of the least safe places to be during a thunderstorm is in the middle of an open field. You should never shelter from a storm by standing beneath a tree, either. The tree can act as a very good conductor of electricity because it is often the tallest thing around.

To cut down the risk of being struck by lightning, it is best to stand away from other people, crouch down low to the ground, keep your head low, and keep both feet together. Lying down, or lying spread-eagled, can also reduce the chances of becoming a target. People have also been struck by lightning while inside buildings because lightning can come down a chimney or through a gap in the roof.

ACTIVITY 7
RAINBOWS

Rainbows, orange-red sunsets, blue skies, and halos are spectacular and colorful effects that result from sunlight being refracted, reflected, or scattered by tiny dust particles or water droplets in the air.

In the 17th century the English scientist Isaac Newton (1642–1727) discovered that white sunlight is really a mixture of light of different colors. He shone a small beam of sunlight through a triangular glass prism (a glass block) in a darkened room. The shape of the prism made the beam of light bend and then split into a broad band of light. In this band Newton identified seven colors, called the spectrum. These colors are red, orange, yellow, green, blue, indigo, and violet.

All light travels as a wave. The length of the wave is what determines the color of the light. Red light has the longest wavelength, orange the next longest, and so on until violet, which has the shortest wavelength of all colors in the visible spectrum.

A rainbow shows all the colors of the light spectrum. Raindrops in the air reflect and bend sunlight to make red, orange, yellow, green, blue, indigo, and violet.

When sunlight passes through a raindrop, the light is bent, or refracted, toward the middle of the raindrop, which splits the white light into all the colors of the spectrum. The separate colors then reflect off the back of the raindrop and separate even more when they leave it. As a result, the light seems to bend into a curve of color, a rainbow. The lights with the shortest wavelengths, such as violet, are on the inside of the curve, and those with the longest wavelengths, the reds, are on the outside. Sometimes a second, faint rainbow can be seen above the main rainbow because the light has been reflected and refracted more than once inside the raindrops. In this second rainbow the colors are reversed, with red on the inside and blue on the outside. The colors are never as bright as the main rainbow because each time light is reflected, a little more is lost.

In 1852 the German scientist Ernst von Brÿcke suggested the blue color of the sky was due to particles in the atmosphere, which diffused, or spread, the sunlight as it entered the atmosphere. Then, two English physicists, Lord Rayleigh (1842–1919) and John Tyndall (1820–1893) came up with another explanation. Rayleigh thought the blue part of sunlight was scattered by dust and water vapor, but he was wrong. It is the air molecules themselves that scatter light. Nevertheless, we still call this type of scattering the Tyndall effect, or Rayleigh scattering, after the two scientists.

Molecules of air scatter the blue light that is present in sunlight the most, making the sky appear blue.

Blue light has the shortest wavelength and is scattered the most by air molecules—almost 10 times as much as the longer wavelengths of red light. During the day we see the blue scattered light as the color of the sky.

As the Sun sets, the sky becomes red because the Sun's rays pass through a much greater thickness of atmosphere than they pass through when the Sun is high in the sky during the day. The blue light is scattered out of the light path, and we see the redder wavelengths. Blue light is also scattered by the particles as the rays travel through this greater thickness of atmosphere, but more red light can be seen.

Rainbows and other light effects in the sky are caused by the light refracting and bending off particles. In the following activities you can make your own rainbows and find out why the sky is sometimes blue or red.

Circular rainbow

If an object is positioned at just the right angle between the Sun and a cloud, it is sometimes possible to see a shadow of that object cast on the cloud. This rare sight is called a brocken specter and is most often seen from airplanes and high on mountain tops.

The brocken specter often appears frighteningly huge because it seems to be much farther away than it really is. The brocken specter is sometimes surrounded by a colorful glowing ring, or halo, called a glory. If the specter is the shadow of a person, the glory appears around the head like a halo.

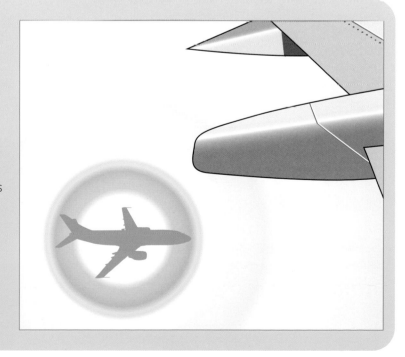

Making Rainbows

ACTIVITY

Goals

1. **Re-create the scattering of light by the atmosphere that makes blue sky and red sunsets.**

2. **Discover why the sky is sometimes different colors at different times of the day.**

What you will need:

- *flashlight with a narrow beam*
- *4 to 6 glue sticks*
- *white background (paper, wall, or cloth)*
- *clear tape*
- *2 polarizing filters*
- *assistant*

1 Shine the flashlight into one end of a glue stick. Hold the other end of the glue stick approximately ½-inch (1 cm) from the white background. Notice that the end of the glue stick closest to the flashlight is a different color from the end nearer the white background. Notice the color of the circle on the white background.

Safety tip

Never shine a flashlight into a person's eyes. The light is very bright and can damage their eyes or yours.

2 Place two glue sticks end to end, and join them together with the clear tape.

3 Repeat step 1, and notice any difference in the colors along the glue sticks and in the colored circle on the white background. You can tape even more glue sticks together and repeat step 1. How do the colors change as you add more glue sticks?

Memory help

There are many different memory aids, or mnemonics, to help you remember the order of the colors in a rainbow. One of them is the name ROY G. BIV (first letters of red, orange, yellow, green, blue, indigo, violet).

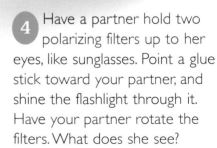

4 Have a partner hold two polarizing filters up to her eyes, like sunglasses. Point a glue stick toward your partner, and shine the flashlight through it. Have your partner rotate the filters. What does she see?

5 If you only have one polarizing filter, hold it between the glue stick and the flashlight, and rotate it. One person should look at the filter from the side.

FOLLOW-UP Making rainbows

Sometimes, the Sun seems to have a halo, or ring, around it. This effect is caused by the bending of the light by tiny ice crystals that are present in the air. Halos can be seen most often when there is a thin layer of cirrus clouds (thin, wispy clouds) over the Sun. Remember, never look at the Sun directly—it will damage your eyes.

The Moon sometimes has a deep blue ring around it, which often has a red outer edge. It is called the lunar corona and is caused by water droplets forming thin cirrus clouds in the sky that bend the light.

You can make your own halo, or lunar corona, with the following activity.

For this experiment you will need a baking tray, water, a flashlight, the use of a freezer (ask an adult first if it is okay to use the freezer), and a helper.

1 Half-fill the tray with water. Do not overfill the tray, since you will have to carry it to the freezer without spilling any. Place it in the freezer and leave it for several hours until the water is frozen solid.

2 Remove the tray from the freezer, and gently remove the ice sheet from the baking tray. The ice will be very cold, so wear gloves to protect your fingers. Wearing gloves will also keep the ice from melting too quickly.

3 Hold the ice sheet, and have your partner shine a flashlight from behind it in a darkened room. Does the reflection of the flashlight on the ice have a halo? What happens as the ices starts to melt and run down the sheet of ice? Is there a new effect?

ANALYSIS

Rainbows

The flashlight emitted light containing all the colors of the rainbow. The glue stick scatters blue light more than yellow or red light. Because the first color to be scattered is blue, the end of the glue stick nearest the flashlight appears blue, while the other end is yellow or yellow-orange. As more glue sticks are joined together, more yellow light is scattered, and the colored circle changes to orange.

Light waves from the Sun, or from an artificial light source such as a flashlight, also vibrate and radiate outward in all directions. When the vibrations are lined up, the light is said to be polarized. You can see an example of natural polarization every time you look at a lake. The reflected glare off the surface is the light that does not make it through the "filter" of the water and is the reason why you often cannot see anything below the surface even when the water is very clear.

Polarized filters contain molecules that are lined up parallel to each other. A polarized filter passes only the light that matches its orientation. Scattering can also polarize light. When you placed a polarizing filter between the flashlight and the glue stick, the top person should have seen a bright beam, while the side person sees a dim beam.

When you hold the polarizing filter between your eye and the glue sticks and rotate it, the filter polarizes the light and so does the scattering. When the two polarizations are aligned, the beam will be bright; when they are at right angles, the beam will be dim.

The glue stick model demonstrates why the sky is blue and why sunsets are red. The sky is blue because blue light is most readily scattered from sunlight in the atmosphere, just as blue light is most readily scattered from white light in the glue sticks. If blue light was not scattered in the atmosphere, the Sun would look a little less yellow and a little more white, and the rest of the sky would be black. At

A glorious sunset of yellows, reds, and oranges. These colors result because the Sun's rays have to travel through a greater thickness of atmosphere.

sunset the Sun is low near the horizon, and light travels through a greater thickness of atmosphere before reaching your eyes than it does when the Sun is higher in the sky. Just like the light traveling along the glue sticks got redder as the glue stick path lengthened.

Sundogs

Tiny ice crystals in the air can cause many strange effects in the sky. Sometimes a multicolored halo or ring forms around the Sun or the Moon because the light is bent (refracted) and reflected by the ice crystals. Often within the halo around the Sun there are two bright spots or patches, one on either side of the Sun, called sundogs or mock suns. The tiny ice crystals have hexagonal (six-sided) faces, and they fall through the air with their flat sides horizontal (straight across). Light refracts through the crystals, splits into the colors of the rainbow, and forms the sundogs.

ACTIVITY 8
WIND DIRECTION

Wind is not something you can see, but you can see what it does as it sets trees and clothes fluttering. And you can certainly feel wind—a warm breeze ruffling your hair or a cold wind freezing your ears.

The winds that blow around Earth do so because of the simple rule that hot air rises. The Earth heats the air immediately above it. As a region of warm air rises, the cooler air that surrounds it flows in to replace it. The cooler air is heated in turn and rises, and is itself replaced by cool air. This type of air circulation is called convection.

Earth is constantly being heated by the Sun's rays, but the Sun does not heat all Earth's surface equally because the planet's surface is curved. Near the equator the Sun's rays hit Earth straight on and

The way that this tree is growing shows us the direction of the prevailing wind—onshore. As the tiny sapling grows, it is always pushed in the same direction, so the adult tree bends as it grows.

are therefore more concentrated, but above and below this region the rays spread out. The heat of the Sun at the equator causes the warm air in that area to rise. As the air rises upward and away from the surface, the pressure of the air is reduced. This means that the equator is an area of low pressure.

When the air reaches the upper atmosphere, it spreads out toward the north and the south. The Sun's rays are weakest at the North and South Poles. The land there is always cold, and the sea is frozen. There the air cools and sinks again. As the air sinks, it contracts, or presses down, creating areas of high pressure. The air above the ice caps is constantly being cooled, and areas of very high pressure develop over the polar regions. Winds are the result of the movement of air from an area of high pressure to an area of low pressure.

WIND SYSTEMS

Weather features such as depressions (an area of pressure lower than its surroundings, which can bring hurricanes in the tropics, for example) do not stay in one place. They move across Earth in the same direction as the main winds that are blowing. These winds are called the prevailing winds and include the trade winds and the westerlies (see page 50). High above these winds are narrow bands of very strong winds called jet streams. These jet streams are often the reason that some weather formations, such as depressions, start to happen. They are often used by high-flying aircraft to speed their journeys. Jet streams are at their strongest during the winter months. That is because very

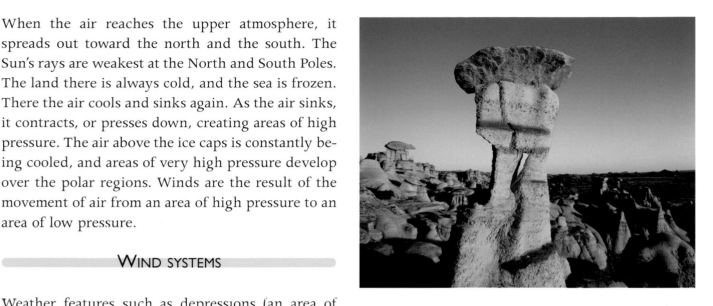

Winds can erode rocks to leave pillars or arches. This pillar has a cap of harder rock that has prevented the softer rock right underneath it from being blown away.

cold air sweeps from the polar regions and forces its way toward the opposite hemisphere of Earth. Some of the jet-stream winds have been measured with speeds up to 200 miles per hour (322km/h).

Other air currents include thermals. They are currents of warm air that rise. Glider pilots and birds look for thermals to help them glide and soar through the air. You can find out the direction the wind near you is blowing in this activity.

Wind power

People have always used wind power. Sailboats rely entirely on wind power to cross oceans. Windmills use wind power to grind grain to make flour. Modern windmills are now built that produce electricity. Wind has many leisure uses as well— sailing, paragliding, windsurfing, and kite flying (right) all rely on a good wind. In fact, kite design has often been used to test new sail and windmill designs.

Making a Weather Vane

Goals

1. **Make a weather vane.**
2. **Use your weather vane to show wind direction.**

What you will need:

- *5-foot (150cm) long wooden dowel*
- *aluminum tray*
- *piece of balsa wood 4 feet (120cm) long*
- *tack*
- *metal washer*
- *white glue*
- *colored cardboard*
- *scissors and pencil*
- *compass*

1 Use the scissors to cut a piece of balsa wood about 2 feet (60cm) long.

2 Use a pencil to mark an arrow-head and a tail shape on the aluminum pie plate (see shapes in picture 3, below). Cut the shapes out using the scissors. Make sure that they are large enough to catch the wind.

Safety tip

Always take care when using scissors and tacks. Make sure an adult is present when you use any tools or sharp objects.

3 Use the scissors to cut a small, vertical slit in each end of the piece of balsa wood. The slits need be about ½ inch (1cm) deep. Put some glue on one slit, and push the triangle into the slit. Repeat with the tail. Put the structure to one side to dry for at least an hour.

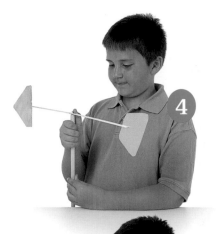

4 Push a tack all the way through the midpoint of the piece of balsa wood. Place the washer on the end of the dowel, and push the tack through the balsa wood and the washer into the top of the dowel. Turn the balsa wood around several times to make sure that it spins freely.

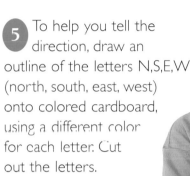

5 To help you tell the direction, draw an outline of the letters N,S,E,W (north, south, east, west) onto colored cardboard, using a different color for each letter. Cut out the letters.

6 Cut four pieces of balsa wood, each 6 inches (15cm) long. Glue one letter to each strip of balsa wood, and glue the wood strips onto the dowel. Make sure you leave the entire instrument to dry for at least an hour.

7 Take your weather vane outside. Use a compass to find which direction is north. Push your weather vane into the ground with the letter N facing north. The arrowhead should point in the direction the wind is blowing from. Record the wind directions each day.

FOLLOW-UP Making a weather vane

You could decorate your weather vane by cutting a shape out of a piece of colored board and stapling it onto the dowel (right).

Keep a record each day to see which way the wind is blowing. It is also important to note what else the weather is doing on that day. Is it nice weather? Is it stormy? What is the temperature?

Check to see when the wind changes direction, and what conditions may have brought about this change.

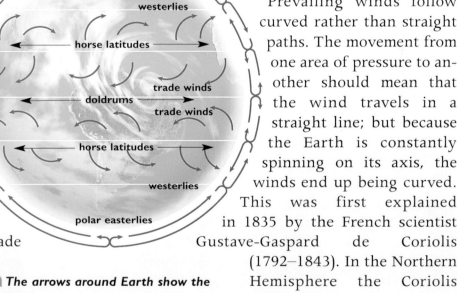

You can also try moving your weather vane to different locations to see if the wind direction changes. The higher up the weather vane can be placed, then the better the results. In some locations there may be trees, bushes, or buildings in the path of the wind. That could affect the wind direction. You can also keep notes of whether the wind changes direction during the day.

ANALYSIS

Wind direction

Wind will always flow from an area of high pressure (where the air is colder) to an area of low pressure (where the air is warmer). This movement of air from high pressure to low pressure creates all the winds that blow over Earth.

In the days when all ships relied on winds, certain areas became known for winds that always blew in the same direction. These winds are called prevailing winds.

Some winds were used to power routes for trading ships, so the winds that blow toward the equator are known as the trade winds. Prevailing winds that blow from west to east are called westerlies. Cold winds from the poles are called

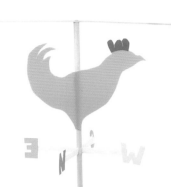

polar easterlies. The area of low pressure near the equator, where winds seldom blow, was called the doldrums. Calm air is also found in areas of high pressure called the horse latitudes.

Prevailing winds follow curved rather than straight paths. The movement from one area of pressure to another should mean that the wind travels in a straight line; but because the Earth is constantly spinning on its axis, the winds end up being curved. This was first explained in 1835 by the French scientist Gustave-Gaspard de Coriolis (1792–1843). In the Northern Hemisphere the Coriolis effect makes winds blow northeast to southwest.

🔲 *The arrows around Earth show the prevailing wind patterns, while the curve of the arrows shows the Coriolis effect.*

ACTIVITY 9
MEASURING WIND SPEED

As the winds move across Earth, they gather force and speed. Strong winds power sailboats and windmills, but they can also bring storms. Measuring wind speed helps predict storms and protect people.

The strength of the wind has a large effect on our lives. While a cool breeze can be very pleasant on a hot day, strong winds often bring storms that can cause great damage.

Wind speed changes frequently, both throughout the year and from place to place. Wind speed is affected both by large-scale climate changes and by local "micro" climates. Some areas of the world, such as the South Pacific, are under constant threat from strong winds and storms. The faster wind blows, the more force it has, and the more damage it can cause. For this reason storms, such as thunderstorms, tornadoes, and hurricanes, are categorized according to how strong the wind is, rather than how much rain they bring.

Winds are categorized on a scale called the Beaufort scale (see page 55), which ranges from Force 0 (complete calm) to Force 12 (hurricane). Studying wind strengths and wind patterns helps meteorologists predict when storms are going to happen and issue storm warnings.

Scientific instruments for measuring exact wind strength have been in use since at least AD 1450. At that time sailors had a particular interest in knowing the wind speed so they could determine when there was enough wind to allow them to leave port, or when a big storm was coming.

■ *This 1989 satellite photo shows Hurricane Hugo heading toward the southern United States.*

More than 2,000 years before this the ancient Chinese determined wind strength and speed by flying huge kites shaped like socks—windsocks. A floppy windsock indicated a light wind, while a strong wind filled the sock with air.

In 1846 the Irish astronomer Thomas R. Robinson (1792–1882) invented a device, the anemometer, for accurately measuring wind speed. This anemometer used spinning cups mounted on the end of arms to catch the wind. The arms turned a shaft as they spun and recorded the wind speed. The design of the anemometer has not changed very much since 1846. In the activity on the following pages you will make your own simple anemometer.

Anemometer

Goals

1. **Build an anemometer and use it to measure wind speed.**

What you will need:

- *4 Styrofoam cups*
- *paint*
- *paintbrush*
- *scissors*
- *thin wooden strip about 18 inches (50cm) long*
- *wooden dowel approximately 18 inches (50cm) long*
- *ruler*
- *pencil*
- *washer*
- *5 thumbtacks*
- *stopwatch*

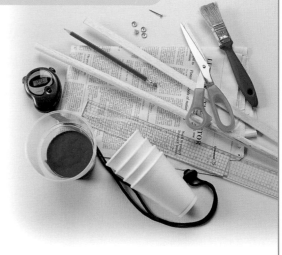

1 Place newspaper on your work surface to protect it, and paint the outside of one of the styrofoam cups.

2 Cut the wooden strip exactly in half. Measure the midpoint of each piece of wood, and mark it with an X, using the pencil. Now, place the two Xs over each other, and put a tack through both pieces of wood.

3 Pin the cups to the ends of the wood strips. Make sure all the cups face in the same direction.

4 Place a washer on top of the piece of dowel, and push the thumbtack in the wooden strip into the top of the dowel. The washer will act as a spacer to make sure the cups can revolve.

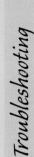

Troubleshooting

What if the cups do not revolve? Test your anemometer before you use it. Blow on the cups to make sure that the cross spins. If it does not spin, pull the thumbtack out slightly. You also need to make sure each arm of the cross is exactly the same length; otherwise your anemometer will not be completely accurate.

5 Take your anemometer outside to a place where you would like to measure the wind speed. Push the anemometer into the dirt, or tie it to a fence. Make sure the cups can spin freely.

Strong wind

The highest wind speed over ground ever recorded was 231 mph (371 km/h), at Mount Washington (altitude 6,288 feet/1,916m), New Hampshire, on April 12, 1934. The windiest place on Earth is Commonwealth Bay, George V Coast, Antarctica, where wind speeds often reach 199 mph (320km/h).

6 Measure the wind speed by counting the number of times the colored cup revolves in one minute. (It is easier with two people—one person timing and one person counting.) That will tell you the wind speed in revolutions (turns) per minute.

◀ 53 ▶

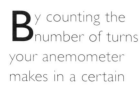

FOLLOW-UP

Anemometer

By counting the number of turns your anemometer makes in a certain period of time, you can create your own wind scale. Measure the wind speed in the same place over several days, or compare wind speeds in different places. Does the wind speed change very much from day to day and from place to place?

You can use your anemometer to determine exact wind speed, but you will need the help of an adult with a car, a wind-free day, and a quiet, deserted road or parking lot.

Have the adult drive the car slowly, at a constant speed, while you hold your anemometer out of the window (always wear your seat belt, and do not stick your arm out of the window). Count the number of turns that the cups make in one minute. That will tell you how many turns of your anemometer are equal to the speed of the car. For example, if the anemometer turns 20 times at 10 mph, that means that 20 revolutions per minute are equal to a wind speed of 10 mph.

ANALYSIS

Measuring wind speed

Although your anemometer cannot withstand very high winds, it is a useful tool for measuring the changes in wind speed. By taking measurements at different times of the year and in different places, you should be able to build up an accurate picture of wind patterns in your area. If you do that, you should find that the wind speed is stronger at certain times of the day and at certain times of the year. That

🔲 *Powerful storms like hurricanes can destroy houses and boats, and flatten trees over miles of area.*

happens because of temperature changes throughout the day and the year. Warm weather heats the air, causing it to rise and create wind. During the day the Sun warms the air, so there tends to be more wind during the day than at night.

Similarly, global wind speed often follows patterns determined by local air temperatures. For example, hurricanes always start over the oceans in tropical and subtropical areas. In different parts of the world these tropical storms have different names: in the Atlantic Ocean they are called hurricanes; in the Pacific Ocean they are called typhoons; over the Indian Ocean they are called cyclones; and when they blow over the northern part of Australia, they are called willy-willies. Hurricanes draw their power from warm and very humid air, which is only found over the warm oceans. For a hurricane to form, the temperature over the ocean must be more than 80°F (27°C). The temperature causes a large amount of water to evaporate from the ocean. Hurricanes grow and develop in the deep layer of humid air that forms just above the ocean.

Hurricanes only start at certain times of the year. In the Northern Hemisphere they start when the heat from the Sun is greatest, from August to October. In the Southern Hemisphere they form between December and May for the same reason.

Tornadoes, or twisters, are also specific to certain places and certain times of year. There is a part of the United States known as tornado alley that is especially prone to tornadoes. Tornado alley covers parts of the Mississippi, Ohio, and Missouri river valleys, although, at certain times of the year tornado alley can extend from Texas to Nebraska and Iowa.

Tornadoes form from summer thunderstorms. Occasionally a long line of 50 or more thunderclouds, or cumulonimbus clouds, will develop. It is called a squall line. A squall line can also contain rotating thunderstorms called supercell thunderstorms. As they rotate, an area of strong low pressure forms. It sucks in other winds, which are rotating around the outside of the storm. As the winds are sucked in, they reach speeds of up to 340 mph (500km/h), creating a whirling funnel of cloud. The funnel of cloud grows longer and longer until it reaches the ground. The low pressure at the center of the tornado creates suction, and the swirling funnel of the twister sweeps along the ground, sucking up everything in its path like a giant vacuum cleaner hose.

Beaufort scale

In 1838 the British Admiral Sir Francis Beaufort (1774–1857) devised a system to group winds according to their strength. He created 13 separate categories and explained what effect they would have on a fully rigged "man-of-war" sailing ship. The scale was based on the amount of sail the ship could carry at different levels of wind. The 13 categories (below) have since been adapted for use on land.

Beaufort Number	Wind Speed (miles per hour)	Description
0	<1	Calm
1	1–3	Light air
2	4–7	Light breeze
3	8–12	Gentle breeze
4	13–18	Moderate breeze
5	19–24	Fresh breeze
6	25–31	Strong breeze
7	32–38	Near gale
8	39–46	Gale
9	47–54	Strong gale
10	55–63	Storm
11	64–75	Violent storm
12	>75	Hurricane

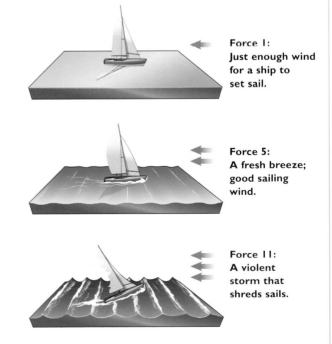

Force 1:
Just enough wind for a ship to set sail.

Force 5:
A fresh breeze; good sailing wind.

Force 11:
A violent storm that shreds sails.

ACTIVITY 10
AIR PRESSURE

Air exerts a force on Earth's surface. We call this force air pressure, and it is important in determining the weather. Measuring air pressure with a device called a barometer can tell us if the weather will be fair, rainy, or stormy.

Watching a stone, or even a piece of paper, fall to the ground, it is hard to believe that air actually exerts a force. Yet the air all around us is constantly pushing in every direction. The force of the pressure is about the same as an elephant standing on a coffee table. Yet we don't feel this pressure because there is an equal pressure inside our bodies pushing out.

People used to think that the pressure of the air, called air pressure, was the result of all the air above us pushing down. Scientists now know that the pressure really comes from the constant bombardment of air molecules as they race around in every direction.

The higher above sea level we go, the less pressure there is. That is because the higher up you go, the fewer air molecules there are. The highest air pressure is felt below sea level.

Air pressure changes with changes in temperature. If the air is cold, it sinks, creating a higher pressure. Warm air rises making areas of lower pressure. Because warm air evaporates faster than cold air to form more clouds, lower pressure is often a sign of an approaching storm. That is why changes

● *Air pressure is usually measured with a barometer (left). A flexible wall in this barometer deflects with changes in air pressure, moving the needle.*

in air pressure can be used to predict the weather. These changes are often measured by using a device called a barometer.

The first barometer was invented in 1643 by the Italian scientist Evangelista Torricelli (1608–1647). He noticed that changes in air pressure always accompanied changes in the weather and that a fall in air pressure signaled a coming storm.

Most barometers give their readings in units called millibars (mb, or bar, for short). Readings over 1,020 mb signal high pressure, while readings of 1,000 mb or below mean low pressure.

PRESSURE AND WEATHER

Air moves from areas of high pressure to areas of low pressure. This movement is wind. High-pressure areas are sometimes called anticyclones. The air in anticyclones is slowly sinking, getting warmer and drying out. This means that the weather will be warm and dry.

A low-pressure area is called a depression. Here the air is rising and cooling and starting to form clouds and rain. Depressions bring with them wet and sometimes stormy weather.

The area where the warm, dry air of an anticyclone meets the cold, wet air of a depression is called a front. Clouds form along the front as the heavier cold air forces itself under the warm air. There are three types of fronts: warm, cold, and occluded. In a warm front warm air moves forward, pushing the cold air ahead of it. Layered clouds and steady rainfall occur on the cold side of the front. When heavier cold air forces itself underneath the warm air, a cold front is formed. As the warm air is pushed up, rain clouds form. An occluded front occurs when a cold front overtakes a warm front. The colder, thicker air cuts underneath the warm air, which rises up and away from Earth's surface, leading to lower temperatures along the front.

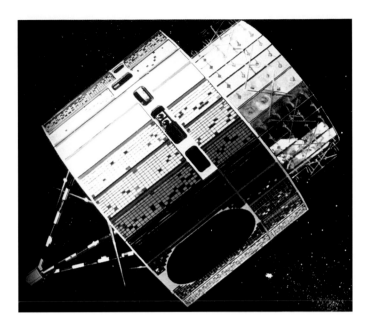

■ *Scientists use weather satellites, like this one, to peer down on Earth and get a more accurate picture of global weather patterns.*

Weather maps

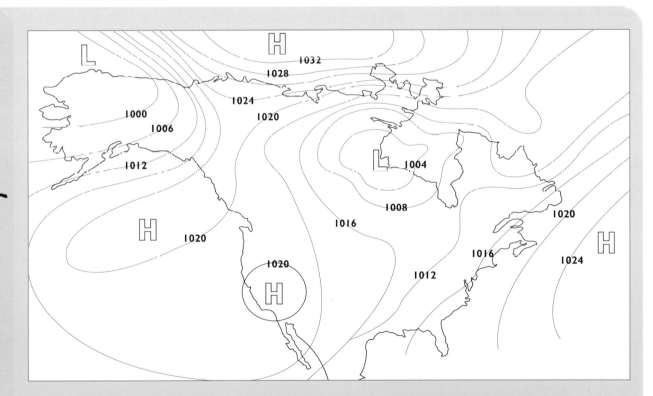

Weather maps like the one above are drawn to show the areas of high (H) and low (L) pressure. On weather maps all the areas of equal pressure are joined to make a curving line called an isobar. Areas of high and low pressure can then easily be identified. The air pressure, in millibars, is marked on each isobar. The map here shows the air pressure over the United States on a particular day. Maps like this are issued each day by the National Weather Service.

Build a Barometer

Goals

1. **Make a working barometer to measure air pressure.**
2. **Predict the weather from changes in pressure.**

What you will need:

- *posterboard*
- *scissors*
- *pen*
- *ruler*
- *plastic plate*
- *tape*
- *balloon*
- *glass*
- *straw*
- *glue/double-sided tape*

1 Cut a strip of posterboard 3 inches (7.5cm) wide and about 8 inches (20cm) long.

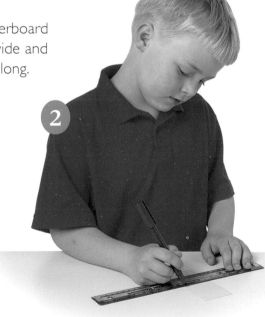

2 Using the ruler and pen, mark lines on the posterboard every ¼ inch (6mm), starting 3 inches (7.5cm) from the bottom. Number each line.

3 Bend the posterboard over 1 inch (2.5cm) from the bottom to make an L-shape. Cut a slit in this bend (this will make it easier to tape). Tape the strip of posterboard onto the plate.

4 Cut the narrow end off the balloon.

5 Stretch the balloon over the glass so that the top of the glass is completely covered, and the balloon is tight.

6 Cut the straw so that one end is pointed. Place a dab of glue on the blunt end of the straw, and lay it on the balloon. Make sure at least 5 inches (12.5cm) of the straw hang over the side of the glass.

7 Place the barometer on the plate so that the pointed end of the straw overlaps the card. Observe your barometer several times each day. Record the position of the straw, as well as the time of day, in your notebook.

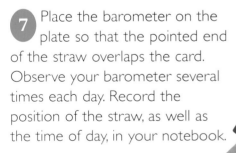

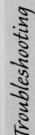

Troubleshooting

What if the straw does not move at all?

It is possible that the air pressure has not changed significantly. Depending on the time of year, the air pressure may remain stable for long periods. Make sure the balloon is absolutely tight across the top of the glass. Try to keep the barometer out of hot direct sunlight since it will heat the air inside, causing it to expand and produce false readings.

FOLLOW-UP

Build a barometer

Record the different readings for your barometer each day. Next to them in your notebook you should also record what the weather was like each day. Use the two measurements to keep track of how the pressure readings on the barometer are related to the weather conditions in your area. Did the pressure reading drop when a storm was approaching?

Did it rise when the weather was nice? Move the barometer around. Does it make a difference if you take the readings inside or outside?

Having made all the equipment in this book—the hygrometer, the anemometer, the weather vane, and the barometer, you now have the tools that weather forecasters regularly use. By taking measurements every day with all

your equipment, and recording the results over a period of weeks or months, you can build up a detailed picture of the weather patterns in your area. Use this information to try to predict the weather. Compare your own weather forecasts with those on TV, in the newspapers, or on the Internet. Are your predictions of the weather more or less accurate than those of the professional meteorologists?

Another barometer

There are many different designs for barometers that you may like to try constructing. They all work on the same principle. The barometer below is even simpler than the one you built in the main activity. Make the barometer below, and compare it with your first barometer. Which one gives more accurate readings?

You will need:
empty plastic soda bottle
washable marker
large glass
water
food coloring

1 Pour water in the glass. Add a few drops of food coloring to the water. That will make it easier to see the water level.

2 Place the bottle upside down in the glass. Make sure the water just enters the mouth of the bottle. Mark the water level in the bottle by drawing a line on the side of the glass using the washable marker. Put the date and time next to the line.

3 Record the water level several times a day. Make sure you label each line with the date and time. You can erase the lines and start again every few days.

4 Measure the water levels. When there is high pressure, the water level should rise. When there is low pressure, the water level should fall. Compare your readings to the weather forecast.

ANALYSIS
Air pressure

In the main activity the air inside the glass is sealed off from the outside air, and so the pressure inside the glass does not change. So, as the outside air pressure increases, it pushes down on the balloon and this raises the straw. When the air pressure drops again, the straw sinks back down.

The barometer in the follow-up works the same way. When the air pressure is high, it pushes down on the water in the glass, forcing more water into the bottle. A high water level in the bottle means high air pressure. When the air pressure is low, it does not press down as hard on the water in the glass, so less water enters the bottle.

If you go on a camping trip to the mountains, you may want to take one of your barometers along with you and measure the air pressure at a higher altitude. The higher up you go, the fewer air molecules there are, so the lower the air pressure will be. Above 16,400 feet (5,000m) the air is so thin that it is very difficult to breathe. If you already live in the mountains, try taking your barometer with you the next time you go to the beach. You should notice a much higher air pressure.

With your weather-forecasting equipment you can make your own weather station. There are more than 5,000 professional weather stations around the world. At each one data is collected using the same type of equipment that you have made.

Professional weather forecasters also collect data from a chain of weather satellites that circle Earth at heights of between 500 miles (800km) and 700 miles (1,100km). The satellites take photographs and collect other data, which is then sent back to Earth and analyzed. The information helps scientists understand how weather in one part of the world can affect weather far away.

Weather balloons

More than 1,000 weather stations around the world send up weather balloons (above) to collect information. Weather forecasters use air pressure to carry these balloons up to the stratosphere, about 20 miles (30km) above the ground. The weather balloons are only partially filled with gas when they are launched. As they rise higher into the atmosphere, the decreasing pressure causes the small volume of gas inside the balloon to expand. The balloon continues to inflate and rises until it reaches the required height. Each balloon carries instruments on board for collecting important data about the weather.

GLOSSARY

advection current: An air current that moves across the ground in a horizontal direction.

advection fog: Thick fog that forms when warm, moist air moves across cooler water or land.

anemometer: A device for measuring wind speed.

anticyclone: An area of high air pressure.

atmosphere: Layer of gas that surrounds a planet.

barometer: A device used to measure air pressure.

blizzard: Heavy snowfall in very windy conditions.

cirrus cloud: Wispy high clouds, sometimes called mare's tails. Cirrus clouds are a sign of nice weather.

cold front: A boundary between air masses where cold air moves forward.

condensation: The process of turning from a gas (such as water vapor) into a liquid.

cumulus cloud: Clouds that look like cotton wool. Made by rising warm air.

cyclone: The name given to hurricanes that occur over the Indian Ocean.

depression: An area where air pressure is lower than it is in the surroundings.

dew: A layer of small drops of water that settles on cool surfaces in early morning.

dew point: The temperature below which the air is too cold to hold water vapor.

doldrums: Areas of low pressure near the equator where winds seldom blow.

drought: A period of inadequate rainfall.

equator: An imaginary line that forms a great circle around Earth halfway between the North Pole and the South Pole.

flash flood: A sudden flood caused by heavy rain falling on hard, dry ground.

flood plain: A flat area of ground around a river over which the river sometimes floods.

fog: Concentration of water droplets in the air near the ground.

front: Boundary where two air masses of different temperatures meet.

frost: Frozen dew.

horse latitudes: Areas of calm in the tropics.

humidity: The amount of water vapor in the air.

hurricane: A tropical storm over the Atlantic Ocean in which the wind speed is force 12, or greater, on the Beaufort scale.

hygrometer: An instrument that measures the amount of moisture in the air.

isobar: A line on a weather map that joins places where air pressure is the same.

jet stream: A narrow band of very strong wind high in the atmosphere.

lenticular cloud: A lens-shaped cloud.

lightning: A powerful discharge of electricity during a storm.

lightning conductor: A metal rod used to divert lightning away from a building by providing a more direct route to the ground.

low: Another name for a depression.

low-pressure area: An area where air rises upward from the ground.

microclimate: The climate of a small area.

mist: A concentration of water droplets in the air near the ground.

monsoon: Very heavy rain that falls for weeks after a dry season in tropical countries.

occluded front: A boundary between two air masses where a cold front overtakes a warm front.

polar easterlies: Cold winds that blow from the North and South poles.

porous material: Any material that has tiny holes (pores) that allow water to pass through.

precipitation: Water falling to the ground as rain, snow, sleet, or hail.

prevailing wind: The main wind at a given place.

prism: A transparent solid used to separate light.

radiation fog: Type of fog formed at night in cool areas near the ground.

rain shadow: The sheltered back slope of a mountain that gets little rain.

reflection: Light "bounced" back off the surface of water, glass, and the like.

refraction: Light deflected as it passes through water, glass, air, and so on.

relative humidity: Measure of how much water the air is holding as water vapor at a given temperature.

saturated ground: Ground that cannot hold any more water.

spectrum: Band of colors— red, orange, yellow, green, blue, indigo, violet— produced when light shines through a prism.

squall line: A line of 50 or more cumulonimbus clouds.

stratus cloud: Cloud that forms a thick layer. Stratus cloud is a sign of drizzle or light rain or snow.

supercell thunderstorm: A type of rotating thunderstorm found in a squall line.

thermal: A current of warm air rising upward.

thunder: The noise of the shock wave made when lightning heats and expands the surrounding air.

tornado: A high-speed, destructive, whirling funnel of cloud reaching to the ground that forms in a supercell thunderstorm. Parts of the American Midwest suffer tornadoes.

tornado alley: That part of the Mississippi, Missouri, and Ohio valleys that is prone to tornadoes.

trade winds: The winds that blow regularly toward the equator. The trade winds were relied on by merchant sailing ships.

twister: Another name for a tornado.

typhoon: The name given to a hurricane that occurs in the Pacific Ocean.

warm front: A boundary between air masses where warm air moves forward.

wind: The movement of air from an area of high pressure to an area of low pressure.

wind-chill factor: The equivalent temperature in still air that would have the same effect on human skin as a higher temperature combined with wind.

SET INDEX